T0378713

SCIENTIFIC AMERICAN EDUCATIONAL PUBLISHING

SCIENTIFIC AMERICAN INVESTIGATES LIFE CYCLES
THE STRANGE LIFE CYCLE OF A CUCKOO

ANNA MCDOUGAL

SCIENTIFIC AMERICAN EDUCATIONAL PUBLISHING

Published in 2025 by The Rosen Publishing Group
in association with Scientific American Educational Publishing
2544 Clinton Street, Buffalo NY 14224

Copyright © 2025 Rosen Publishing Group

Library of Congress Cataloging-in-Publication Data
Names: McDougal, Anna, author.
Title: The strange life cycle of a cuckoo / Anna McDougal.
Description: Buffalo, NY : Scientific American Educational Publishing,
   [2025] | Series: Scientific American investigates life cycles | Includes
   bibliographical references and index.
Identifiers: LCCN 2024008054 (print) | LCCN 2024008055 (ebook) | ISBN
   9781725350854 (library binding) | ISBN 9781725350847 (paperback) | ISBN
   9781725350861 (ebook)
Subjects: LCSH: Cuckoos–Life cycles–Juvenile literature.
Classification: LCC QL696.C83 M423 2025 (print) | LCC QL696.C83 (ebook) |
   DDC 598.7/4–dc23/eng/20240312
LC record available at https://lccn.loc.gov/2024008054
LC ebook record available at https://lccn.loc.gov/2024008055

Portions of this work were originally authored by Barbara M. Linde and published as *The Bizarre Life Cycle of a Cuckoo*. All new material in this edition authored by Anna McDougal.

Designer: Tanya Dellaccio Keeney
Editor: Caitie McAneney

Photo credits: Cover Peter Garrity/Shutterstock.com; p. 5 (top) Arcadio Marin/Shutterstockc.com; p. 5 (bottom) Dennis W Donohue/Shutterstock.com; p. 7, 9, 11 (top) Vishnevskiy Vasily/Shutterstock.com; p. 11 (bottom) penphoto/Shutterstock.com; p. 13 green scent/Shutterstock.com; p. 15 Rafal Szozda/Shutterstock.com; p. 17 Kevin Manns/Shutterstock.com; p. 19 Romuald Cisakowski/Shutterstock.com; p. 21 alsamua/Shutterstock.com.

All rights reserved. No part of this book may be reproduced in any form without permission in writing from the publisher, except by a reviewer.

Printed in the United States of America

CPSIA compliance information: Batch #CSSA25. For Further Information contact Rosen Publishing at 1-800-237-9932.

CONTENTS

THE CURIOUS CUCKOO 4

ONCE UPON A NEST 6

STEALING HOME 8

BIRD BABYSITTERS 10

BEGGING FOR FOOD. 12

TIME TO FLY! 14

ALL AROUND THE WORLD 16

ON THE HUNT. 18

SAVE THE CUCKOOS! 20

GLOSSARY .22

FOR MORE INFORMATION 23

INDEX 24

Words in the glossary appear in **bold** type the first time they are used in the text.

THE CURIOUS CUCKOO

Have you ever seen a cuckoo clock? Have you ever heard someone call something "cuckoo"? The cuckoo is a bird. More than 125 species of cuckoo live around the world. Some cuckoos are small birds, while others grow up to 36 inches (91 cm) long!

You may have never seen a real cuckoo. That's because they are shy birds. They like to hide in areas thick with trees. However, there's one thing they're not shy about. They borrow other birds' nests! This is one strange part of their life cycle.

Yellow-billed cuckoos have loud calls. They're sometimes called a "rain crow," because some people think they're calling for rain.

FUN FACT

THE CUCKOO FAMILY INCLUDES ROADRUNNERS, A FAST GROUND CUCKOO WITH A LONG TAIL.

ONCE UPON A NEST

Different kinds of cuckoos have different **habitats** and **behaviors**. However, they all start as an egg. Some of them, such as the yellow-billed cuckoo, build nests and hatch their own young. A male and female yellow-billed cuckoo build a nest made of twigs and grass.

The female lays up to five eggs. Then, the male and female yellow-billed cuckoos take care of the eggs together. After about 10 days, the eggs hatch. Chicks leave the nest after about a week.

Baby cuckoos—called hatchlings—have no feathers. Feathers grow a few days after they hatch.

FUN FACT

SPECIES SUCH AS YELLOW-BILLED CUCKOOS AND ROADRUNNERS CARE FOR THEIR OWN YOUNG.

7

STEALING HOME

Some cuckoo parents feed their own babies in their own nests. However, some kinds of cuckoos have a different plan. They don't raise their own babies. Instead, the female lays her eggs in the nests of other birds! These kinds of cuckoos are called **brood** parasites. Parasites depend on other creatures, without giving anything in return.

First, the cuckoo makes a fuss so the **host** mother bird will leave her nest. Then, the cuckoo lays her egg in the host mother's nest. Sometimes she lays eggs in multiple nests.

This cuckoo egg makes itself at home in a Marsh warbler's nest. Can you tell which egg is different from the rest?

FUN FACT

THE CUCKOO MAY PUSH THE HOST'S EGGS OUT OF THE NEST OR EVEN EAT ONE TO MAKE ROOM FOR HER EGG.

BIRD BABYSITTERS

What if a host bird doesn't want to care for a cuckoo baby? Cuckoos trick them. The cuckoo's eggs **mimic** the host bird's eggs, though they may be larger. The female cuckoo often lays her eggs in the nests of the same kind of bird that raised her.

Sometimes, the host bird recognizes the cuckoo's egg and leaves it to start a new nest. More often, the host bird sits on all the eggs. The cuckoo egg hatches first, sometimes a whole day before the other eggs.

FUN FACT

THE EGGS OF A COMMON CUCKOO ARE LIGHT BLUE-GREEN AND SPOTTED.

This common cuckoo chick is in a marsh warbler nest.

11

BEGGING FOR FOOD

Baby cuckoos are masters of mimicry too. To get its host mother to feed it, a cuckoo chick mimics the cries of the other baby birds. The baby cuckoo tosses other eggs or chicks out of the nest to get more food. Even then, the host mother still feeds the cuckoo!

A young cuckoo eats whatever the host mother gives it. This may be beetles, grasshoppers, or fruit. Once the chick is old enough, it leaves the nest. Then it's time to join its own kind.

This host bird mother is much smaller than the cuckoo chick it's caring for!

FUN FACT

CUCKOOS STAY WITH THEIR HOST BIRD FOR ABOUT TWO WEEKS, GROWING MUCH BIGGER IN THAT TIME. THEY BECOME FLEDGLINGS.

TIME TO FLY!

Cuckoos continue to grow. They work on their flying skills. Some even **migrate** when they're big enough. The cuckoo's strange life cycle doesn't stop after the chicks leave the nest. They also have a strange ability to follow their cuckoo parents without any directions!

Some cuckoos fly to warmer areas for the winter and then fly back again. Some stay within one country. Others fly thousands of miles, even from one **continent** to another.

> Cuckoos sometimes fly nonstop for weeks at a time.

FUN FACT

THE COMMON CUCKOO IS ONE MIGRATING SPECIES. BORN IN EURASIA, IT SPENDS ITS WINTERS IN WARMER PLACES IN AFRICA AND EVEN EAST ASIA.

ALL AROUND THE WORLD

Cuckoos build their homes all over the world. For some, their habitat is a deep forest. Others live in fields. Cuckoos can be found in both cold and warm **climates**.

Some kinds of cuckoos like trees, and some kinds like to stay on the ground. Cuckoos commonly live alone, though. When they're old enough, they will come together to mate, or make babies. Then, the female cuckoo lays an egg. The life cycle begins again!

Cuckoos hide so well in their habitats, it's more common to hear a cuckoo call out "cu-coo" than to see the bird.

FUN FACT

YELLOW-BILLED CUCKOOS BUILD NESTS HIGH IN TREES—SOMETIMES 90 FEET (27.4 M) OFF THE GROUND!

ON THE HUNT

Cuckoo chicks are helpless when they are born. Their parents or host mothers bring them food. Over time, they learn to hunt. Adult cuckoos are insect hunters. Hairy caterpillars are a favorite cuckoo food. Luckily for the cuckoos, most other birds don't eat these caterpillars!

To catch a caterpillar, the cuckoo sits on a branch. It watches the grass and leaves below. When a caterpillar moves, the cuckoo pounces. It grabs the caterpillar in its beak. Cuckoos eat caterpillars in one big gulp!

If a cuckoo swallows too much caterpillar hair, it can throw up its whole stomach lining and replace it!

FUN FACT

HAIRY CATERPILLARS ARE HARD TO EAT! CUCKOOS SHAKE AND ROLL EACH CATERPILLAR IN THEIR BILL BEFORE SWALLOWING IT. THIS TAKES OFF MANY OF THE HAIRS.

SAVE THE CUCKOOS!

Cuckoos are smart birds. Some have found a way to trick others into caring for their young! However, they face dangers. Some cannot find enough bugs to eat because of **pesticides** used by farmers. Cuckoo mothers may have trouble finding places for their eggs as trees are cut down. Some may have trouble migrating across growing deserts.

Cuckoo populations are going down. Some people think they need to be protected. These birds need our help to keep living for years to come!

Some cuckoos lay eggs in their own nests like normal birds. Others find smart ways to give the work of child-rearing to someone else!

LIFE CYCLE OF A CUCKOO

- EGG
- HATCHES
- HATCHLING
- LEAVES NEST
- FLEDGLING
- GROWS
- ADULT
- MATES

GLOSSARY

behavior: The way an animal acts.

brood: A group of young birds or other animals hatched or born at the same time to one mother.

climate: The average weather conditions of a place over a period of time.

continent: One of Earth's seven great landmasses.

Eurasia: Europe and Asia considered together.

fledgling: A young bird that has just grown flight feathers or learned to fly.

habitat: The natural place where an animal or plant lives.

host: An animal or plant that provides for another kind of animal or plant.

migrate: To move from one area to another for feeding or having babies.

mimic: To look or sound like someone or something else.

pesticide: Something used to kill pests, such as unwanted bugs.

FOR MORE INFORMATION

Books

Nelson, Louise. *Life Cycles*. Minneapolis, MN: Jump!, Inc., 2024.

Zambello, Erika. *Backyard Birding for Kids: An Introduction to Ornithology*. Cambridge, MN: Adventure Publications, 2022.

Websites

Cuckoo
kids.britannica.com/kids/article/cuckoo/353024
Explore more fun facts about the cuckoo.

Yellow-Billed Cuckoo
www.allaboutbirds.org/guide/Yellow-billed_Cuckoo/overview#
Learn more about the yellow-billed cuckoo and listen to its call.

Publisher's note to educators and parents: Our editors have carefully reviewed these websites to ensure that they are suitable for students. Many websites change frequently, however, and we cannot guarantee that a site's future contents will continue to meet our high standards of quality and educational value. Be advised that students should be closely supervised whenever they access the internet.

INDEX

adult, 18, 21

brood parasites, 8

call (birdsong), 5, 17

diet, 12, 18, 19

eggs, 6, 8, 9, 10, 11, 12, 16, 20, 21

endangered, 20

fledgling, 13, 21

flying, 14, 15

habitat, 6, 14, 16, 17

hairy caterpillars, 18, 19

hatchling, 7, 21

hunting, 18

mimicry, 12

nests, 4, 6, 8, 9, 10, 12, 21

pesticides, 20

physical description, 4, 5

roadrunner, 5, 11

species, 4, 11, 15

trees, 4, 17, 20

yellow-billed cuckoo, 5, 6, 7, 17